W9-CLJ-059

Into the Earth

Into *the* Earth

The Story of Caves

By Meredith Costain

NATIONAL GEOGRAPHIC

WASHINGTON D.C.

One of the world's largest nonprofit scientific and educational organizations, the National Geographic Society was founded in 1888 "for the increase and diffusion of geographic knowledge." Fulfilling this mission, the Society educates and inspires millions every day through its magazines, books, television programs, videos, maps and atlases, research grants, the National Geographic Bee, teacher workshops, and innovative classroom materials. The Society is supported through membership dues, charitable gifts, and income from the sale of its educational products. This support is vital to National Geographic's mission to increase global understanding and promote conservation of our planet through exploration, research, and education.

For more information, please call
1-800-NGS-LINE (647-5463) or write to the following address:
National Geographic Society
1145 17th Street N.W.
Washington, D.C. 20036-4688
U.S.A.

For information about special discounts for bulk purchases, please contact
National Geographic Books Special Sales at ngspecsales@ngs.org

Visit the Society's Web site: www.nationalgeographic.com

Copyright © 2006 National Geographic Society

Text revised from *Caves* in the National Geographic Windows on Literacy program from National Geographic School Publishing, © 2004 National Geographic Society

All rights reserved. Reproduction of the whole or any part of the contents without written permission from the publisher is prohibited.

Published by National Geographic Society. Washington, D.C. 20036

Design by Project Design Company

Printed in the United States

Library of Congress Cataloging-in-Publication Data

Costain, Meredith.
Into the earth : the story of caves / by Meredith Costain.
    p. cm. – (National Geographic science chapters)
Includes bibliographical references and index.
ISBN-13: 978-0-7922-5950-3 (library binding)
ISBN-10: 0-7922-5950-5 (library binding)
1. Caves. I. Title. II. Series.
GB601.C66 2006
551.44'7--dc22
                    2006016325

Photo Credits
Front Cover: © National Geographic Image Collection; Spine: © Stuart Wilson/ Eye Ubiquitous; Endpaper: © Raymond Gehman/ National Geographic Image Collection; 2-3: © Stuart Wilson/ Eye Ubiquitous; 6: © APL/ Corbis; 7: © Bill Hatcher/ National Geographic Image Collection; 8: © Dave Bunnell; 12-13: © D Brown/ PanStock/ Panoramic Images/ National Geographic Image Collection; 14: © Dave Bunnell; 15: © Tom Bean/ Stone/ Getty Images; 16: © Stephen Alvarez/ National Geographic Image Collection; 17: © APL/ Corbis; 19: © Stephen Alvarez/ National Geographic Image Collection; 20: © Joseph H. Bailey/ National Geographic Image Collection; 21 (left): © Mary Ann McDonald/ Corbis; 21 (right): © Jodi Cobb/ National Geographic Image Collection; 22 (inset): © Joel Sartore/ National Geographic Image Collection; 22-23: © Tim Laman/ National Geographic Image Collection; 23 (bottom): © Stephen Alvarez/ National Geographic Image Collection; 24: © Stephen Alvarez/ Stone/ Getty Images; 25 (top): © Lynda Richardson/Corbis; 25 (bottom): © Dietmar Nill/ Nature Picture Library; 26: © Gary Braasch/ Corbis; 28: © Eddie Soloway/ Stone/ Getty Images; 29: © Robert Cameron/ Stone/ Getty Images; 30: © Chris Johns/ National Geographic Image Collection; 31: © Dave Bunnell; 32: © Arne Hodalic/ Corbis; 34: © Stephen Alvarez/ National Geographic Image Collection; 35: © Carsten Peter/ National Geographic/ Getty Images; Illustrations by Dimitrios Prokopis.

Contents

A man crawls
through a small
opening in a cave.

Into the Earth

Imagine crawling on your hands and knees in the dark. The ground is hard. You are covered in mud. You are cold and wet. It doesn't sound like much fun, but it is. What you are doing is both dangerous and exciting. You are exploring a cave.

Two cavers examine a pool deep within a cave.

Chapter 1

Inside a Cave

A cave is a hollow space under the ground.
Caves are also called caverns. Caves can be
found all over the world. You can find them
on the side of a mountain, inside huge pieces
of ice, or even in lava.

Some caves are small holes or tunnels
beneath the ground. Other caves are made
up of many chambers, or large open spaces.
Narrow tunnels connect the chambers.
Caves that have many chambers are called
cave systems.

**A caver explores a huge cave in Tennessee. This cave system
is more than 33 miles (53 km) long.**

How Caves Are Formed

Caves are mostly found in a soft rock called limestone. Rainwater trickles down through tiny cracks in the rock. Over hundreds of thousands of years, the rainwater wears away the limestone, forming a cave.

3. After thousands of years, tunnels and chambers form.

4. If enough water enters a cave, a stream can form.

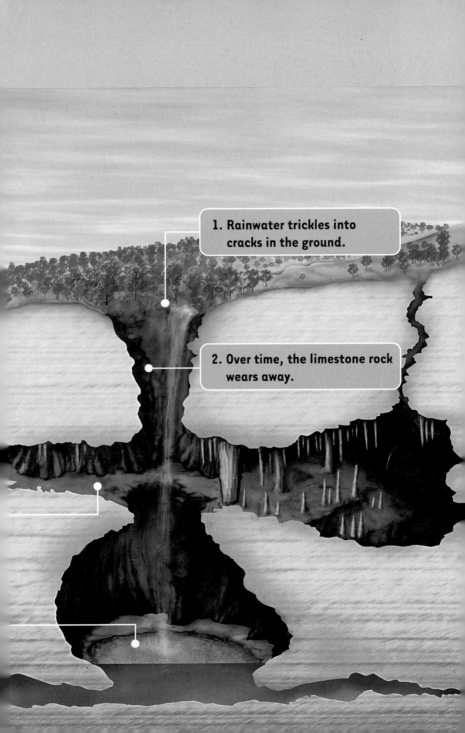

1. Rainwater trickles into cracks in the ground.

2. Over time, the limestone rock wears away.

Rock Formations

Once inside the chamber of a limestone cave, the first thing you'll notice are the many beautiful rock formations. In many caves, pointy fingers of rock hang down from the ceiling. Rock formations that hang from the

Many different kinds of rock formations can be seen in Carlsbad Caverns in New Mexico.

ceiling of a cave are called stalactites. These rock icicles form when limestone mixes with water and trickles through cracks in the ceiling of a cave. It can take thousands of years for a stalactite to form.

stalactite

column

stalagmite

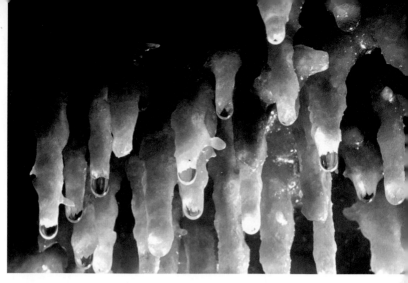

You can see the drops of water ready to drip off newly forming stalactites.

Stalagmites are rock formations that grow on the floor of a cave. Stalagmites form when water trickles down the side of a stalactite and drips onto the cave floor. Over time, the stalagmite becomes a pointy peak sticking out of the cave floor.

If water continues to seep into a cave, a stalactite and a stalagmite will eventually meet in the middle. When this happens, they form a rock formation known as a column.

◀ The rock formations in a cave are continuously changing.

Chapter 2

Life in a Cave

Caves can be home to many types of animals. Plants live in caves, too. The types of plants and animals you can find in a cave depend on where in a cave you are. The plants and animals that live near a cave entrance are very different from those that live deep within a cave in total darkness.

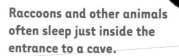

Raccoons and other animals often sleep just inside the entrance to a cave.

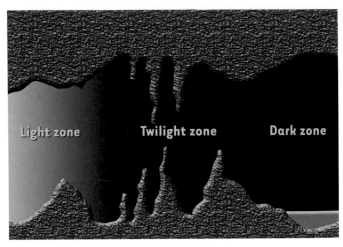

The deeper you go into a cave, the darker it gets.

Scientists divide the area within a cave into three zones, or parts. The entrance to a cave is known as the light zone. This part of a cave receives some sunlight.

As you travel farther into a cave, it becomes much darker. It also becomes much cooler. This part of a cave is known as the twilight zone.

Deep inside a cave is the dark zone. No light reaches the dark zone. It is always dark, damp, and chilly in the dark zone.

Natural light does not reach far within a cave so few plants grow there.

A sloth bear emerges from its den inside a cave.

The Light Zone

Leafy plants, such as ferns, grow easily in the light zone at the entrance to a cave. Some animals, such as bears and bobcats, use caves for shelter. Most of the animals that live in the light zone are visitors. They spend part of the time outside the cave.

▼ Ferns often grow near a cave entrance.

▲ A bobcat takes shelter in a cave.

Bats sleep during the day and hunt for food at night.

The Twilight Zone

As you go farther into a cave, the light becomes dim. The temperature gets much cooler. Plants, such as mosses, that don't need much light grow in the twilight zone. Bats sleep during the day in the darkness of the twilight zone. Other animals, including the cave salamander, live on the wet rock walls.

Cave salamanders eat insects they find on wet rock walls.

Blind crayfish use their antennae
to feel their way in the darkness.

▲ Isopods are very small water animals that live in the darkness.

▶ Olms are a kind of salamander that live deep within a cave.

The Dark Zone

The area deep inside a cave is called the dark zone. No plants grow here, but some animals live their entire lives in the dark zone.

Most of the animals that live in the dark zone are blind because no light ever reaches them. Some creatures, such as the olm, don't even have eyes. Olms have a very good sense of hearing to make up for not being able to see. Isopods and other small water animals have feelers to help them move about.

Chapter 3

Types of Caves

Most caves form when rainwater wears away limestone rock. However, there are other ways that caves can form. Caves can be found in ice, along the coast, and even in lava.

Ice Caves

Caves can be found inside gigantic, slow-moving pieces of ice called glaciers. These kinds of caves are called ice caves. As a glacier melts, a stream of water flows underneath it. Together, the water and warm air hollow out the ice to form a cave.

A man stands in a huge ice cave.

Waves wash in and out of sea caves along the coast.

Sea Caves

Caves sometimes form along the shores of oceans and large lakes. Pounding waves break away loose rock on a cliff. Over thousands of years, the strong waves carve out a sea cave. The cave continues to grow until the waves can no longer reach deep within the cave.

It can be wet or dry inside a sea cave, depending on the time of day and time of year. Unlike limestone caves, sea caves rarely have rock formations in them. They are, however, home to many sea animals. The only way to explore these caves is to swim into them or take a small boat.

The force of waves battering against a cliff can cause sea caves to form.

Lava Tube Caves

Volcanoes create some caves. When a volcano erupts, red-hot lava flows down the sides of the mountain. The side of the lava closest to the air cools and hardens into rock. The lava underneath continues to flow. The flowing lava leaves behind a long, hollow tube with smooth sides. These tubes are known as lava tube caves. Lava caves can be up to 40 miles (64 km) long.

Lava swirls before flowing into the ocean near a village in Hawaii.

The longest lava tube cave
in the world is in Hawaii.

Two spelunkers climb though a cave tunnel.

Chapter 4

Spelunking

Exploring caves is a popular hobby. In the United States, it is called spelunking. Spelunking is fun, but it can be dangerous, too. Spelunkers need to wear warm clothing that they don't mind getting dirty. Most wear a helmet with a light attached. This enables them to see in the dark without having to hold onto a flashlight.

Spelunkers explore in groups. They make a map of the cave as they go. Each member of the group has a buddy who can get help if someone is injured. Having a buddy also prevents people from getting lost inside a cave.

Spelunkers need to be careful that the
caves and the animals that live in them are
not harmed. Spelunkers have a saying:

*"Take nothing but pictures,
leave nothing but footprints,
kill nothing but time."*

◀ A spelunker squeezes her way through a tight passage.

▼ Spelunkers often use ropes to lower themselves into a cave.

How to Write an A+ Report

1. Choose a topic.
- Find something that interests you.
- Make sure it is not too big or too small.

2. Find sources.
- Ask your librarian for help.
- Use many different sources: books, magazine articles, and websites.

3. Gather information.
- Take notes. Write down the big ideas and interesting details.
- Use your own words.

4. Organize information.
- Sort your notes into groups that make sense.

- Make an outline. Put your groups of notes in the order you want to write your report.

5. Write your report.

- Write an introduction that tells what the report is about.

- Use your outline and notes as you write to make sure you say everything you want to say in the order you want to say it.

- Write an ending that tells about your report.

- Write a title.

6. Revise and edit your report.

- Read your report to make sure it makes sense.

- Read it again to check spelling, punctuation, and grammar.

7. Hand in your report!

Glossary

cavern	a large cave
cave system	a collection of caves linked by tunnels
chamber	a large open space in a cave
column	a rock that forms when a stalactite and stalagmite join together
erupt	to explode or burst out
glacier	a large piece of ice that moves slowly aross the land
lava	the hot liquid rock that comes out of a volcano
limestone	a soft, white, chalky rock
spelunking	exploring caves
stalactite	a rock formation that grows downward from the ceiling of a cave
stalagmite	a rock formation that grows upward from a cave floor

Further Reading

• Books •

Nonfiction

Allman, Toney. *Life in a Cave (Ecosystems)*. San Diego, CA: Kidhaven Press, 2004. Ages 9-12, 48 pages.

Aulenbach, Nancy Holler, and Hazel A. Barton, with Marfe Ferguson Delano. *Exploring Caves: Journeys Into the Earth*. Washington, DC: National Geographic Society, 2001. Ages 9-12, 64 pages.

Davis, Wendy. *Limestone Cave (Habitats)*. New York, NY: Children's Press, 1998. Ages 9-12, 32 pages.

Lauber, Patricia. *Painters of the Caves*. Washington, DC: National Geographic Society, 1998. Ages 10-14, 48 pages.

Lindop, Laurie. *Cave Sleuths: Solving Science Underground*. Minneapolis, MN: Twenty-first Century Books, 2004. Ages 9-12, 80 pages.

Fiction

Skurzynski, Gloria, and Alane Ferguson. *Running Scared (Mysteries in Our National Parks, Book 11)*. Washington, DC: National Geographic Society, 2002. Ages 9-12, 160 pages.

• Websites •

Public Broadcasting Service
http://www.pbs.org/wgbh/nova/caves/

National Speleological Society
http://caves.org/

National Caves Association
http://cavern.com/

The Caving Pages
http://www.cavesource.com/

Glossary of Speleological and Caving Terms
http://werple.net.au/~gnb/caving/glossary/

Index

RECEIVED JUL 07 2014